Updated Las Vegas Travel Guide 2023

Discover the Ultimate Guide to Sin City: Your Complete Las Vegas Travel Companion for 2023

Alyssa Hickman

Copyright © 2023 Alyssa Hickman

Table of Contents

Map of Las Vegas

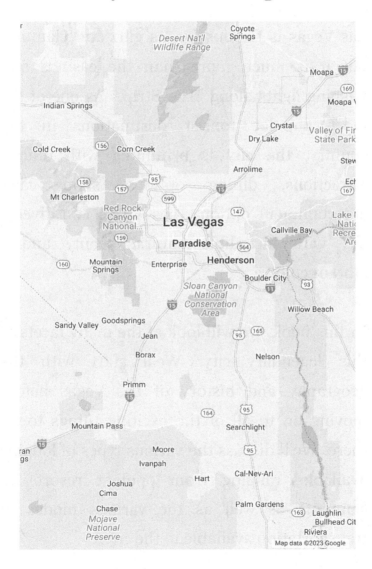

Introduction

Las Vegas is famous for its glitz and glamour, but it is much more than the casinos and flashing lights along "The Strip." As one of the most popular tourist destinations in the country, the city is brimming with unique attractions, dining options, shops, and entertainment options. Las Vegas is a diverse city with incredible natural beauty and a vibrant culture.

In this book, we will look at the many facets of this legendary city. We'll start with the geography and history of Las Vegas before moving on to all of the exciting things to do there. We'll discuss the various types of lodging available, ranging from opulent resorts to camping, as well as the various modes of transportation available in the city.

We will also visit the must-see attractions in Las Vegas, such as the famous Strip and the breathtaking Red Rock Canyon. Before we look at some of the possible day trips, we'll take a look at the city's safety and security features. Finally, we will reflect on our exploration of Las Vegas and make some recommendations for future exploration.

This book will provide you with all of the information you need to plan an unforgettable trip to Las Vegas. Let's get started!

Chapter 1: Introduction to Las Vegas

Overview of Las Vegas

Las Vegas is a lively and exciting city known for its bright lights and nonstop entertainment. However, few people are aware of the city's rich history. Las Vegas, located in Nevada's Mojave Desert, has been a settlement for a long time and has seen many changes.

The Paiute tribe was the first known group to live in the Las Vegas area before the first European settlers arrived in the 1800s. They had lived in the area for many years. Following the arrival of Mormon settlers in the area in 1855, Las Vegas was established as a settlement in 1905 and was granted city status in 1911.

Because of its legalized gambling, entertainment, and nightlife, Las Vegas grew to become a popular tourist destination throughout the twentieth century.

Las Vegas is now one of the most popular tourist destinations in the United States. The city has many casinos, hotels, restaurants, and other attractions that offer a variety of entertainment. Las Vegas is also an important financial and business center, with a thriving service, travel, and gaming economy.

Conventions, conferences, and other events are held frequently in Las Vegas. The city is home to the world's largest convention center, where many of the world's largest corporations hold their events.

In Las Vegas, visitors can find a wide variety of bars, nightclubs, and other venues that provide a variety of entertainment. The nightlife in Las Vegas is well-known. In addition, the city hosts numerous festivals, events, and concerts, providing visitors with a diverse range of entertainment options.

In addition to entertainment and nightlife, Las Vegas has a variety of cultural pursuits. Visitors can explore the city's museums, galleries, and other cultural institutions, in addition to its beautiful parks and outdoor recreation areas.

History of Las Vegas

The sprawling gambling mecca of Las Vegas is located in the Mojave Desert of southwest Nevada. It is one of the country's most recognizable cities, distinguished by its brilliant neon lights, opulent casinos, and extravagant shows. However, Las Vegas's history is far more nuanced and fascinating than its current reputation would suggest.

Native American tribes first settled in what is now Las Vegas thousands of years ago, and Spanish missionaries later explored it in the early nineteenth century. They began a mission there, but it was soon terminated. The area was then settled by a variety of people, including Mormons and ranchers, who established small settlements.

When Las Vegas was incorporated as a city in 1905, it was the ideal location for a railroad town. The city grew quickly around the Union Pacific Railroad, which had recently laid tracks through the area. Las Vegas quickly became popular as a tourist destination as well as a hangout for organized crime figures.

When gambling became legal in the state of Nevada in 1931, Las Vegas grew rapidly. Casinos and hotels began to spring up all over the city, and the famous Las Vegas Strip became a popular tourist destination. The city was also known for its lavish entertainment, which featured top musicians and comedians.

In the late twentieth century, Las Vegas began to diversify its economy and shed its image as the epicenter of gambling. The city attracted several large corporations, and the entertainment and technology industries centered there. Las Vegas has also developed a reputation for having excellent dining, shopping, and nightlife.

Las Vegas is a vibrant, diverse city that is one of the most popular tourist destinations in the United States today.

In this city of extremes, the old and the new coexist, resulting in an intriguing fusion of traditional and contemporary culture. Las Vegas has a rich history that has contributed to its status as an iconic destination. It remains an exciting and adventurous location.

The geographical location of Las Vegas

Las Vegas is geographically located in the Mojave Desert, a region of the southwest United States distinguished by its arid climate and limited vegetation. The surrounding terrain is mostly flat, with a few low-lying mountain ranges providing some elevation. This area is home to a variety of desert animals, including lizards, desert tortoises, and jackrabbits.

The Colorado River, which flows to the city's north, has shaped its geography significantly.

The river provides an important source of moisture to the nearby desert, allowing vegetation to grow and creating a unique microclimate in the city. The river also provides the city with an important source of hydroelectric power, a reliable source of electricity.

Las Vegas is home to the Spring Mountains, a large mountain range. These mountains, which are part of the larger Sierra Nevada mountain range, dramatically frame the city. The mountain range is home to a variety of animals, including bighorn sheep, mountain lions, and mule deer.

The Pacific-North American plate boundary fault is close to Las Vegas. As a result, the city is earthquake-prone, though the likelihood of a major earthquake is quite low.

Las Vegas' geography has been critical to the city's growth. Because of the Colorado River, which provides a consistent source of electricity, the city has grown into a significant hydroelectric power hub. The presence of the Spring Mountains has also attracted tourists and outdoor enthusiasts, making the city a popular destination for skiing, hiking, and camping.

Chapter 2: Exploring the City

Dining and Shopping in Las Vegas

For those looking for a fine-dining experience, Las Vegas has a variety of options. From Michelin-starred restaurants to family-friendly options, there is something for every palate and budget. The Strip is home to some of the world's best restaurants, including Joel Robuchon's Le Cirque and Gordon Ramsay's Pub & Grill. For a more relaxed experience, numerous eateries serve delectable food at reasonable prices. The Grand Lux Cafe at The Venetian, for example, has a large menu that includes everything from traditional Italian dishes to modern favorites.

Las Vegas has an abundance of shopping opportunities. The Grand Canal Shoppes at The Venetian and The Forum Shops at Caesars Palace are two of The Strip's numerous large malls. Furthermore, downtown Las Vegas has a diverse selection of unique shops and boutiques. For those looking for a more diverse experience, the Arts District has several independent stores and galleries.

In Las Vegas, visitors can enjoy a wide variety of attractions and activities. From interactive shows at the various casinos to the internationally renowned Las Vegas Strip, the city has something for everyone. The Bellagio fountain and the "Welcome to Las Vegas" sign are two iconic landmarks that make Las Vegas a truly one-of-a-kind destination.

Entertainment Options

For those who enjoy the high-stakes excitement of a casino, Las Vegas is the ideal destination. Las Vegas is a gambler's paradise, with some of the world's largest casinos, including the Wynn and Bellagio. In addition to table games like blackjack, craps, and roulette, many casinos offer slots, video poker, and other electronic gaming machines. Those who do not want to gamble have many other options for entertainment, such as live performances, concerts, nightclubs, and dining establishments.

Las Vegas is home to some of the world's most well-known performances, including Cirque du Soleil and the Blue Man Group. These shows are a fantastic way to experience the unique atmosphere of Las Vegas while watching a memorable show.

There are also a variety of live music venues available, ranging from tiny bars to massive arenas. You can find anything in Las Vegas, whether it's a jazz performance or a rock concert.

People who enjoy the outdoors will find many natural attractions in Las Vegas. A nearby hiking and picnicking destination, Red Rock Canyon, offers breathtaking views of the desert surroundings. A variety of tours are available to visit the nearby Hoover Dam, a popular tourist destination, and explore the area surrounding the dam.

Las Vegas is also a fantastic shopping destination. The city is home to some of the world's best malls and outlets, as well as a variety of unique shops selling gifts and souvenirs.

Sightseeing

Those who want to explore the city can choose from a variety of sightseeing activities. A ride on the High Roller observation wheel is an excellent way to get a bird's-eye view of the city. For those looking to explore the outdoors, Red Rock Canyon National Conservation Area offers amazing trails, breathtaking views, and a variety of wildlife. For those looking for a more urban experience, the Neon Museum, which is dedicated to preserving the neon signs of early Las Vegas, is a good option.

For those who want to explore the famous Las Vegas Strip, a walking tour is a fantastic way to take in the sights and sounds of the city. A walking tour provides an up-close look at the city, from the iconic Bellagio Fountains to the vibrant energy of the casinos.

Many of the city's performances, including Cirque du Soleil, can also be seen from the Strip.

For those looking for a more unique experience, Las Vegas has many unusual attractions. The Mob Museum, a museum devoted to the history of organized crime, is a must-see for those interested in learning more about the city's seedier side. The Pinball Hall of Fame also houses a large collection of pinball machines dating from the 1950s to the present day.

2.4 Recreational and Outdoor Activities

One of the city's most popular pastimes is visiting famous sights along the Las Vegas Strip. Downtown Las Vegas is home to several unique attractions, including the Bellagio's dancing fountains and a replica of Paris's Eiffel

Tower. The High Roller, for example, is the world's tallest observation wheel and is located in the heart of the Strip. Another popular tourist attraction in Las Vegas is the Neon Museum, which showcases the city's vibrant neon culture.

Las Vegas visitors can engage in a variety of outdoor activities. The Red Rock Canyon National Conservation Area, a popular vacation destination, is only a short drive from the Strip. Visitors can explore the breathtaking desert scenery, participate in outdoor activities such as hiking and rock climbing, or simply enjoy the scenery. It's also worth going to the nearby Valley of Fire State Park, which has geological formations, petroglyphs, and historic ruins to explore.

Las Vegas has a plethora of water-based activities. Visitors can visit nearby Lake Mead or participate in water sports such as kayaking, stand-up paddling, and wakeboarding. The lake, the country's largest reservoir, allows visitors to engage in a variety of leisure activities such as swimming, boating, and fishing.

Chapter 3: Accommodations

Hotels

It's critical to understand that there are numerous types of hotels in Las Vegas, including convention hotels, resorts, and boutique properties. While resorts such as the Mandalay Bay offer a more opulent experience with a wide range of amenities and activities, traditional hotels such as the Bellagio provide tasteful lodging and easy access to the city's attractions. Travelers looking for a more personalized experience can find it at boutique hotels such as the Nobu Hotel.

Whatever the hotel type, Las Vegas is known for its friendly service. The majority of the city's hotels offer amenities such as free parking, breakfast, and Wi-Fi. Furthermore, many hotels offer a variety of amenities such as spas, fitness centers, and swimming pools. Furthermore, many hotels offer special packages for special occasions such as weddings and anniversaries.

The cost of a hotel in Las Vegas can vary greatly. The Travelodge Las Vegas and the Circus Circus are two budget hotels with basic amenities at reasonable prices. The Venetian and the Wynn are two high-end hotels that offer a variety of amenities and services for those looking for a more opulent experience.

In addition to a variety of hotels, Las Vegas is home to several casinos. From the iconic MGM Grand to the iconic Bellagio, Las Vegas is a gambler's paradise. In addition to slots and table games, many casinos provide a variety of entertainment options such as live shows and celebrity appearances.

Last but not least, keep in mind that Las Vegas is also home to many attractions, such as the High Roller and the Fountains of Bellagio. There are also many galleries, museums, and other cultural establishments in the city.

Resorts

First and foremost, Las Vegas resorts come in a variety of sizes and shapes. This city has everything from large, all-inclusive resorts to small, boutique hotels. Visitors to grand resorts with extensive facilities and amenities, such as MGM Grand, The Venetian, and The Bellagio, have access to gaming, spas, swimming pools, and dining options. These resorts frequently offer a variety of room types, ranging from simple rooms to opulent suites and villas. Smaller resorts with fewer amenities, such as The Cromwell and The D Las Vegas, are more intimate and often provide a more personalized experience.

Regardless of the type of resort you choose, you can expect a wide range of amenities and services. The majority of resorts have a variety of restaurants, bars, and nightclubs, as well as a casino and gaming floor. Many resorts also have spas, swimming pools, and fitness centers to help visitors unwind. In addition, some resorts offer additional services such as pet-friendly lodging, concierge services, and transportation.

When selecting a Las Vegas resort, your budget, preferences, and needs should all be considered. Luxury resorts, while typically more expensive, provide superior services and amenities. Smaller resorts may be less expensive, but they may lack the same range of features and amenities. The resort's location, as well as its proximity to points of interest and entertainment, should be considered.

Vacation rentals

Vacation rentals are an excellent choice for a comfortable and stylish way to explore a city. Vacation rentals allow travelers to enjoy all of the amenities of a home away from home while also allowing them to explore and create their own unique experiences.

In Las Vegas, visitors can select from a variety of vacation rental options. From condos to entire houses and villas, travelers can select the ideal size and type of lodging for their needs. Many of these vacation rentals include a full kitchen, living room, and bedroom, allowing visitors to cook and relax in their own private space.

Many rentals include amenities such as pools, hot tubs, and outdoor patios for those looking for a little extra relaxation.

Tourists can save money by choosing rentals over hotels in addition to the added convenience. Vacation rentals are generally less expensive than hotels and provide more space and privacy. For larger groups, a vacation rental can be a cost-effective solution because it allows everyone to stay in the same location while still having their own private space.

When booking a vacation rental in Las Vegas, it is critical to consider the neighborhood. While some rentals are in quieter residential areas, others are near popular attractions, casinos, and entertainment. Even though the majority of vacation rentals are in the city center, there are an increasing number of options outside the city limits. These rentals provide a more private and tranquil setting and are frequently more affordable.

Camping

To the north and east of Las Vegas, the Nevada-Utah border marks the start of the Black Rock Desert, a large area of desert terrain. It has some of the best views in the area, thanks to its rocky outcrops and expansive vistas. The Black Rock Desert is a popular camping destination, with plenty of space to spread out and park RVs. Because there are no facilities on-site, campers should bring their supplies, including food and water.

The Spring Mountains National Recreation Area is another excellent camping spot near Las Vegas. This area, which is only a few miles from the city, has a variety of camping options, ranging from backcountry sites to RV parks. In the area, there are numerous hiking and mountain biking trails, as well as a variety of wildlife to enjoy. There are also many campgrounds with amenities such as bathrooms and electricity in the park.

The Valley of Fire State Park is a breathtaking region of red sandstone and desert beauty located just one hour north of Las Vegas. Numerous rustic campsites in this region offer breathtaking views of the red cliffs and surrounding countryside. Because there is no water in the Valley of Fire, campers should bring plenty of their own.

The Lake Mead National Recreation Area is an excellent choice for campers looking for a peaceful retreat. Lake Mead, located east of Las Vegas, has camping options ranging from beachfront to secluded backcountry. There are numerous activities in the area, such as boating, fishing, and exploring the nearby canyons.

Finally, the Red Rock Canyon National Conservation Area is a fantastic camping spot close to Las Vegas. The region's striking red rock formations provide numerous opportunities for exploration and adventure. Several campgrounds within the park offer both primitive and RV sites.

Chapter 4: Transportation

Getting Around the City

Taking public transportation is the most cost-effective way to get around in Las Vegas. The Regional Transportation Commission of Southern Nevada (RTC) operates a bus, shuttle, and rapid transit network with routes to the airport, the heart of Las Vegas, and the Strip. Prices vary depending on the route but can be quite reasonable. The RTC also offers a variety of discounts and passes to frequent travelers. The disadvantage of public transportation is that it can be slow and unreliable, with long waits between buses.

Taxi is another popular mode of transportation in Las Vegas. Taxis are a dependable and convenient mode of transportation that can get you where you need to go quickly.

Prices vary depending on distance traveled but are typically higher than those for public transportation. Furthermore, some taxi companies may charge extra for services such as luggage handling.

Ride-sharing services such as Uber and Lyft are popular ways to get around in Las Vegas. These services are affordable, flexible, and convenient. Ride-sharing services are typically less expensive than traditional taxi services and can be reserved through a smartphone app. Ride-sharing services may not be available everywhere in the city, and they may not be able to accommodate larger groups or luggage.

Renting a car in Las Vegas is a great way to get around if you want to visit many of the nearby attractions. Car rental companies offer a wide range of vehicles, including compact cars, luxury vehicles, and SUVs. The price is affected by the type of vehicle and the length of the rental period. However, driving in Las Vegas can be challenging, especially when traffic is heavy. Furthermore, parking can be both expensive and difficult to find in some areas.

Walking is a great way to get around in Las Vegas. Walking allows you to explore the city and discover hidden gems, even if it is not the most efficient way to get from point A to point B. When you walk, you don't have to worry about parking or traffic, and it's free. The disadvantage is that it can take a long time, especially if you want to travel a long distance.

Public Transportation

One of the best ways to get around Las Vegas is to take public transportation, which is convenient, inexpensive and can take you to a variety of locations throughout the city.

The Regional Transportation Commission of Southern Nevada (RTCSNV) manages the Las Vegas public transportation system. RTCSNV provides a variety of services, including express routes, rapid transit, shuttles, and buses. Every bus in the system has bike racks and wheelchair access. Senior citizens and people with disabilities can get discounts. The type of service and the number of zones traveled to determine the fare.

The RTCSNV bus system, which operates daily from 5 a.m. to midnight, serves the majority of the city's major attractions, including the Las Vegas Strip, downtown Las Vegas, and the Las Vegas Convention Center. Buses run every 10 to 30 minutes depending on the route.

Furthermore, the RTCSNV operates express routes with fewer stops, which can get you to your destination faster.

The Deuce, a double-decker bus, travels along the Las Vegas Strip. This bus has Wi-Fi and runs 24 hours a day, seven days a week. Because it stops at the majority of the major hotels and attractions on the Strip, the Deuce is an excellent way to travel quickly and conveniently.

The Las Vegas Monorail, which runs along the Strip, connects the major casinos and attractions. Tickets are available at kiosks located at each station, and the monorail operates seven days a week from 7 a.m. to 2 a.m. This is a fantastic option for those who want to avoid the Strip's traffic and crowds.

Aside from buses and the monorail, there are other ways to get around Las Vegas. Taxis are readily available throughout the city, in addition to rideshare services such as Uber and Lyft. Limousines and party buses can be rented for special occasions for those looking for a more unique experience.

Car Rentals

Renting a car is a great way to fully experience Las Vegas and all of its attractions. Renting a car is typically less expensive than taking taxis and more comfortable than taking the bus or train. Furthermore, renting a car allows you to personalize your trip by allowing you to travel at your own pace and explore the city in the way that suits you best.

Before renting a car, there are a few important factors to consider. First, select a vehicle that meets your requirements. Given the size and sprawl of Las Vegas, if you're traveling with a large group or a lot of luggage, you might want to consider a larger vehicle, such as an SUV or van. If you're looking for something more affordable, a compact car or hybrid may be a good option.

It's critical to do your research on the rental car company you choose. The best car rental companies have competitive rates, a large selection of vehicles, and excellent customer service. Additionally, look for companies that offer extra services such as free pick-up and delivery, emergency roadside assistance, and flexible return policies.

It is also critical to understand the rules and laws that govern car rentals in Las Vegas. Drivers under the age of 25 may be charged a surcharge, and all drivers must be at least 21 years old. Most rental car companies also require a credit card, a valid driver's license, and proof of insurance.

Finally, before signing the rental agreement, make sure to thoroughly read it. This ensures that you understand all of the rental agreement's terms and conditions, including any additional fees, fuel policies, and deposit requirements.

Taxis and Ride-sharing

Taxis are an excellent way to get around Las Vegas. Taxis are widely available throughout the city, and hailing one from the street or calling one ahead of time is simple.

You won't need cash because the majority of taxis in Las Vegas accept credit cards. Taxis also provide a more personalized service than ride-sharing services because drivers frequently know the area and can make recommendations or offer advice based on personal experience.

Taxis, on the other hand, can be expensive. Although fares vary depending on distance, traffic, and time of day, fares in Las Vegas are generally higher than those in other cities. Furthermore, if you are traveling during rush hour, you may encounter traffic and a lengthy wait for a taxi.

Uber and Lyft are two popular ride-sharing services that can help you get around Las Vegas. Ride-sharing services are typically less expensive than taxis and more convenient because they can be summoned directly from your smartphone. Furthermore, ride-sharing services frequently offer discounts and promotions, increasing their affordability.

However, ride-sharing services have some drawbacks. There may be a wait for a ride, and some areas may be without ride-sharing services. Ride-sharing services are also not always reliable because drivers may cancel or become disoriented. Finally, because ride-sharing services frequently only seat 4-5 passengers, they may not be suitable for large groups.

When deciding which mode of transportation is best for getting around Las Vegas, it's critical to weigh the advantages and disadvantages of both taxis and ride-sharing services. Although taxis are typically more expensive than ride-sharing services, they provide more personalized service and are easier to summon from the street. Although ride-sharing services are less expensive, they are not always available and are not always the best option for large groups. The best way to get around Las Vegas ultimately depends on your needs and financial situation.

Chapter 5: Must-See Attractions

The Strip

The Strip in Las Vegas, Nevada, is a well-known feature of the American landscape and a symbol of contemporary consumer culture's excess. The four-mile-long Strip runs along Las Vegas Boulevard and is located at the valley's southernmost point. The Strip has served as the setting for numerous stories, both on and off-screen, and is a hub of culture, entertainment, and consumerism.

The Strip is home to some of the most well-known casino hotels in the world. From the iconic Bellagio and its cascading fountains to the lavish gardens of the Wynn, these resorts capture the opulence of the region.

The High Roller, the world's tallest observation wheel, and the Fountains of Bellagio, a choreographed water show, are just two of The Strip's many attractions.

In addition to casinos and attractions, the Strip is lined with numerous dining establishments, nightclubs, and retail establishments. The Strip has a wide range of dining options, including fine dining establishments such as Le Cirque and classic diner-style restaurants such as Heart Attack Grill. The Strip's nightlife is legendary, with legendary venues such as the Mirage's 1 Oak and XS Las Vegas.

Two of the most important events on the Strip are the Electric Daisy Carnival and the World Series of Poker. The Strip is one of the most popular tourist destinations in the world, thanks in part to these events, which attract thousands of visitors each year.

The Strip has long been a symbol of Las Vegas' distinct culture and has aided in the formation of the city's identity. It is home to a diverse range of cultures and people, from glitzy high rollers to the quiet locals who form the city's backbone. It also serves as a gathering place for people of all backgrounds to enjoy the unique fusion of consumerism, culture, and entertainment.

Fremont Street

Fremont Street is a historic street with its distinct charm and personality. The street, which is lined with vintage neon signs in the style of Las Vegas, is an excellent place to learn about and experience the city's history. The Fremont Street Experience, one of the country's longest-running free shows, is also located on this street. This show, which features a brilliantly illuminated light show set to music, is a must-see for anyone visiting the area.

Fremont Street, in addition to providing entertainment, is a fantastic place to eat delicious food. The street is home to a diverse range of dining and drinking establishments, from traditional Las Vegas steakhouses to unique restaurants. There are also numerous unique food carts and trucks serving a variety of street fare.

Taking the Fremont Street Experience is a great way to see the street from a different perspective. A large canopy of LED lights has been installed above the street, creating an intriguing and distinct atmosphere.

This massive light show, which offers an unforgettable experience, is accompanied by live music.

Red Rock Canyon

Red Rock Canyon in Las Vegas is a breathtaking natural formation located just west of the city. It is a distinct desert setting with a variety of stunning landscapes, including high sandstone cliffs, high mountains, and the canyon's well-known red rocks. The canyon is part of the Mojave Desert, which covers 2,900 square miles and is home to a diverse range of wildlife. Hikers, bikers, rock climbers, and other outdoor enthusiasts visit Red Rock Canyon regularly.

The impressive geological formation known as Red Rock Canyon contains an impressive variety of geological features.

The canyon's most prominent feature is its towering red rocks, which are formed from an accumulation of sandstone and other sedimentary rocks. For millions of years, sandstone has eroded, resulting in the formation of red rocks. As a result, the landscape is breathtaking, with high cliffs and unusual formations. Sandstone and limestone formations, as well as a variety of other rock formations, can also be found in the canyon.

The canyon provides important habitat for bighorn sheep, mule deer, desert tortoises, and a variety of other animals. The desert willow and the desert wildflower are just two examples of the canyon's diverse plant life. The canyon serves as a major migration route for many bird species, including the peregrine falcon and the golden eagle.

Furthermore, the canyon is a popular destination for outdoor activities such as camping, biking, rock climbing, and hiking. The canyon is also popular among photographers due to its stunning scenery and vibrant colors. Red Rock Canyon is also popular for stargazing due to its clear skies and night skies.

Hoover Dam

The Red Hoover Dam in Las Vegas is one of the most well-known man-made structures in the world. The dam, located in the Mojave Desert, stands as a testament to human engineering prowess. The Hoover Dam, which was built in the early 1930s, is a magnificent engineering feat that spans the Colorado River and creates the large Lake Mead reservoir. With millions of tourists visiting each year, it has become a popular tourist destination.

The Hoover Dam is a 726-foot-tall concrete arch-gravity structure. It has a length of 1,244 feet and a thickness of 1,244 feet at its base. The dam, which also generated hydroelectric power, was supposed to regulate the flow of the Colorado River. The dam provides water to over 20 million people in Nevada, Arizona, and California. It also generates more than 4 billion kilowatt-hours of hydro electricity per year.

The Hoover Dam is an engineering marvel, but it is also an environmental success story. The dam has helped to prevent erosion and flooding in the area. It has also aided in water conservation for the area's numerous cities and towns. The dam has also been credited as a major factor in the development of the Las Vegas tourism industry. The dam has allowed the city to grow and thrive by providing a reliable and consistent source of fresh water.

Chapter 6: Safety and Security

Crime Prevention

Surveillance is the most widely used method of crime prevention in Las Vegas. Security cameras are installed in many public places, including casinos, hotels, and shopping malls. This allows the police to monitor activity and spot unusual behavior. Furthermore, Las Vegas police are increasingly relying on facial recognition technology to help them identify potential suspects.

To better anticipate potential criminal activity, Las Vegas employs surveillance in addition to predictive policing strategies. In predictive policing, data analysis is used to identify patterns and trends that can help law enforcement focus on neighborhoods where crime is more likely to occur. This strategy has proven to be effective in several cities, including Las Vegas.

In Las Vegas, community policing is an important crime prevention strategy. This strategy entails close cooperation between neighborhood residents and the police to foster trust and a sense of safety in the community. This frequently entails police officers getting to know their neighborhoods and interacting with residents regularly. This strategy is being used in Las Vegas because it has been shown to reduce crime in other cities.

Finally, education is an important aspect of crime prevention in Las Vegas. Many organizations, including the Las Vegas Metropolitan Police Department, provide classes to teach people how to protect their homes, belongings, and communities. These programs frequently emphasize teaching participants how to be more aware of their surroundings and recognize suspicious activity. They also provide useful information on how to report crimes and stay safe.

Emergency Services

Las Vegas Fire and Rescue (LVFR) is the city's primary provider of fire protection, rescue, and emergency medical services. They have cutting-edge firefighting and rescue equipment, such as water tenders, ambulances, ladder trucks, and fire engines. They also provide public education and training on fire safety and prevention.

The Las Vegas Metropolitan Police Department (LVMPD) is the primary law enforcement agency for the city and its environs. They are responsible for responding to and investigating a wide range of crimes, including murders, robberies, drug trafficking, and domestic abuse. The LVMPD also provides support and training to other law enforcement organizations in the city.

The Southern Nevada Health District (SNHD) is a public health organization that provides medical, environmental, and public health services to the city's residents. The SNHD provides immunizations, disease surveillance, public health inspections, and health education. They also deal with public health emergencies and outbreaks such as water contamination and food-borne illnesses.

The three organizations work together to respond to emergencies in a coordinated manner. The LVFR and LVMPD handle the majority of calls, with the SNHD providing technical and medical support. The city also has many volunteer organizations, such as the Las Vegas Fire Corps, that provide additional assistance and materials. These organizations are critical for responding quickly and effectively to any emergency in the city.

Dealing with Unfamiliar Situations

Here are some tips for dealing with unusual situations in Las Vegas.

1. **Research the Area**: Before traveling to Las Vegas, it is critical to learn about the local climate, cultural norms, and popular attractions. As a result of getting to know the city and its surroundings, you will feel more at ease navigating the area.

Also, do some research on the area you intend to visit, such as the casinos and the best routes.

2. **Create a Budget**: Before embarking on your journey, you must first create a budget. You'll be able to stay within your budget while also relaxing and enjoying the experience. Consider setting limits for yourself, such as how much you will bet and how long you will stay out.

3. **Remain Alert**: When you're in an unfamiliar situation, it's critical to be aware of your surroundings. Pay attention to the people around you, and don't be afraid to call the police if you feel unsafe. Additionally, avoid walking after dark or in isolated areas.

4. **Ask for Help**: If you find yourself in an unfamiliar situation, do not be afraid to ask for

help. Tourists in Las Vegas can take advantage of a variety of amenities, such as concierge services and visitor centers. Consider conversing with locals, who can provide useful information about the city and its culture.

5. **Be Prepared**: Finally, be prepared for any situation that may arise. Bring a phone, some cash, and a map; these items will come in handy in an emergency. Consider bringing a first-aid kit and a list of emergency phone numbers.

Chapter 7: Day Trips

Lake Mead

It's a short drive from Las Vegas to Lake Mead. The distance is covered in about an hour, depending on traffic. Travelers will be able to admire the breathtaking desert vistas as well as the majestic mountains, canyons, and other natural features that make up the region's landscape as they travel.

When visitors arrive at Lake Mead, they can choose from a variety of activities. Boating is a popular activity, and a variety of boats are available for rent. Another popular activity is fishing, which allows you to catch a variety of species such as trout, bass, catfish, and bluegill. Visitors can enjoy the lake by swimming, kayaking, paddleboarding, and other water sports.

The lake itself is a stunning sight, with its azure waters and stunning desert setting. Visitors can also observe the diverse local wildlife, which includes birds, lizards, and other creatures. There are also numerous hiking trails to explore, allowing visitors to appreciate the area's stunning natural surroundings.

For visitors who want to make the most of their day trip to Lake Mead, there are numerous nearby attractions to visit. The Hoover Dam is nearby and a popular tourist destination. Visitors can visit the nearby visitor center or take a boat tour of Lake Mead in addition to touring the dam.

Death Valley

The journey begins with a two-hour drive from Las Vegas to the western entrance of Death Valley.

Visitors will be treated to stunning views of the Amargosa Valley, the Panamint Range, and the surrounding desert landscape. Visitors to Death Valley can explore a variety of landscapes, including salt flats and dunes, and see a diverse array of animal and plant life.

One of the most popular things to do in Death Valley is drive along the Badwater Road, a winding road that cuts through the valley's center. From the road, you can see the famous salt flats and the Badwater Basin, as well as breathtaking views of the surrounding area. The Artist's Palette, a vibrant rock formation composed of reds, greens, and blues, is just one of the geological formations found in the valley through which the road travels.

Another popular activity in Death Valley is visiting the nearly 600-foot-deep Ubehebe

Crater. At this impressive site, visitors can explore the crater's rim and get a close-up view of its impressive size.

For those looking for a more leisurely activity, a stroll through the Mesquite Flat Sand Dunes is a fantastic way to take in the scenery and soak up some sun. The dunes are a popular location for photographers because the constantly changing scenery creates a unique backdrop.

Finally, visitors to Death Valley can stop by the Furnace Creek Visitor Center to learn more about the valley's ecology and history, as well as get a close-up view of the surrounding area. Because it also has a variety of exhibits and educational programs, the visitor center is a great place to end the day trip.

Grand Canyon

The journey is relatively simple given that it only takes four hours to drive from Las Vegas to the Grand Canyon. To get to the Grand Canyon's South Rim from Las Vegas, take Interstate 40 East, then Highway 64 South. You can stop along the way to admire the stunning views of the Joshua Tree Forest and the Mojave Desert.

Once you arrive at the Grand Canyon, you can explore the numerous trails and overlooks in the area. There are over 25 trails to explore, ranging from easy strolls to strenuous hikes. Many of the trails offer stunning views of the canyon and its surroundings. If you don't want to hike, there are numerous beautiful overlooks to enjoy.

The Grand Canyon is home to a variety of animals, including bighorn sheep, mule deer, elk, and coyotes. You might be lucky and see one of these creatures while you're there. The park also contains a variety of bird species, including the Mexican jay, American dipper, and California condor.

If you want to spend the night near the Grand Canyon, there are many options. There is something for everyone, whether you want to stay in a luxurious hotel or a rustic cabin. For those who want to stay inside the park, the Grand Canyon Lodge offers a variety of lodging options.

Valley of Fire

The Valley of Fire is a vast expanse of miles of brilliant red rocks formed by iron oxide deposits.

It provides an excellent backdrop for outdoor exploration. Hiking trails wind through the park, providing breathtaking views of the valley. Visitors can also see the numerous petroglyphs carved into the rocks by the region's native inhabitants, as well as the unusual rock formations and stunning desert scenery.

The best way to experience Valley of Fire is on a guided tour. These tours provide visitors with in-depth knowledge of the park's geology, ecology, and history. Tour guides explain the park's unique features, such as the prehistoric fossils found in the rock formations, the unique wildlife that lives nearby, and the park's historical significance.

In addition to the guided tours, guests can explore the park on their own. To explore, there are numerous trails, picnic areas, campgrounds, and visitor centers. For those who prefer a slower pace, there are numerous scenic drives to choose from. Many of the roads are well-kept and provide stunning views of the valley.

Chapter 8: Planning Your Trip

Budgeting for Your Trip

Planning a trip to Las Vegas can be both exciting and difficult. Many factors must be considered when creating a budget for a trip to Sin City, from determining an appropriate spending limit to reserving the ideal accommodations. Make a plan and set realistic expectations to maximize your budget and ensure a successful trip.

The first step in creating a budget for a trip to Las Vegas is determining your spending limit. Consider the cost of travel, lodging, meals, and entertainment. These expenses can quickly add up, so it's critical to create and stick to a reasonable budget.

Consider making some sacrifices to stay within your budget if necessary.

After you've determined your budget, you can begin making hotel reservations. Consider the type of hotel you'd like to stay in and compare your options to find the best deal. It is critical to factor in the cost of transportation to and from your hotel. You might want to consider hiring a car service to and from the airport or renting a car for the duration of your trip.

After you've reserved your lodging, the next step is to plan your meals and entertainment. Do some research on local eateries and attractions to get an idea of the average price. If you want to save money, consider eating at the hotel or participating in free activities such as walking tours or open-air performances.

Finally, while in Las Vegas, it is critical to consider potential supplemental expenses. This can include unanticipated expenses such as car repairs or medical care. Make sure to leave some money in your budget for unforeseen expenses.

Using these steps and considering the cost of each component of the journey, you can budget for a successful and enjoyable trip to Las Vegas. With proper planning and preparation, you can maximize your vacation while staying within your budget.

When to Visit

Las Vegas, known for its exciting entertainment options and vibrant nightlife, is one of the country's most recognizable cities. The city is a popular travel destination for visitors from all over the world, and it is home to some of the world's most renowned casinos. Given the variety of attractions available in Las Vegas, it is understandable that many people wonder when to visit.

The best months to visit Las Vegas are March through May or September through November. The mild weather makes sightseeing and outdoor activities enjoyable during these months. Because the weather is neither too hot nor too cold, visitors can enjoy everything the city has to offer. During these months, visitors can also save money on accommodations because hotel rates typically fall.

Any season is a good time to visit Las Vegas, but the summer and end of the year are the busiest. Summertime in the city is a hive of activity due to the abundance of outdoor activities and attractions.

Because Las Vegas is a fantastic place to celebrate New Year's Eve, the end of the year is also an excellent time to visit. Visitors should plan ahead of time because hotel rates are frequently higher during this time.

Whatever the season, there is always something to do in Las Vegas. There are numerous entertainment options, and the city has some of the world's best dining and nightlife. There is something for everyone, from shows to casinos to outdoor adventures.

When making travel plans to Las Vegas, it is critical to consider factors such as the weather and hotel costs. Visitors can enhance their experience and make the most of their trip by planning ahead of time. Las Vegas is a fantastic destination all year, so make sure to take advantage of everything it has to offer.

How to Get There

Las Vegas, a thriving and exciting destination, has something for everyone. Because of its world-class casinos and entertainment, Las Vegas is a vacation destination unlike any other. If you're planning a weekend getaway or a longer vacation, there are numerous ways to get to Las Vegas and make the most of your time there.

Air travel is one of the most convenient ways to get to Las Vegas. Many airports across the country offer direct and nonstop flights to Las Vegas. Flying is frequently the simplest and most practical mode of transportation, as well as a cost-effective option. Before making your flight reservation, look for discounts or special fares, as many airlines offer them.

If you prefer to travel to Las Vegas by car, you can take a road trip. It's critical to plan your trip carefully because the drive can take anywhere from nine to thirteen hours, depending on where you are. Making stops along the way allows you to break up the journey and take in the sights and sounds of the American West.

If you're looking for adventure, you can take the train to Las Vegas. Amtrak provides routes to Las Vegas from a variety of American cities, some of which offer scenic views of the countryside. Taking the train is an excellent option for sightseeing or escaping the hustle and bustle of the Las Vegas Strip.

Regardless of how you choose to travel to Las Vegas, planning ahead of time is essential. Before you travel, do your research on the location, find lodging, and make reservations.

Make sure you are familiar with the rules and regulations that govern the casinos and other attractions. Although Las Vegas is a thrilling vacation destination, it is critical to use caution and good judgment while there.

Las Vegas is a memorable destination with something for everyone. There are numerous ways to visit Las Vegas and enjoy everything the city has to offer, whether you're planning a quick weekend getaway or a longer vacation. Driving, flying, and taking the train are all options for getting to Las Vegas. Plan ahead of time to make the most of your trip.

Traveling Documents

For good reason, Las Vegas is one of the most popular tourist destinations in the world. With its vibrant nightlife, world-class entertainment, and constantly changing attractions, it's easy to see why the city is so appealing to visitors. However, Las Vegas, like any other tourist destination, requires specific travel documents in order to enter and enjoy the city. In this article, we'll go over the documents you'll need to visit Las Vegas, such as passports, visas, and any other necessary documents.

A valid passport is the first requirement for traveling to Las Vegas. All US citizens traveling to the US must have a valid passport, which is especially important for international travel. A passport is a government-issued document that allows citizens of the United States to travel to other countries. It must be valid for the duration of the journey and presented at the port of entry. Passports must also be renewed every five to ten years, depending on the country that issued them.

A visa may also be required for international travelers. A visa is a government-issued document that allows a foreign national to enter the United States. A visa may be required for both business and leisure travel, depending on the traveler's country of origin. Visas must be obtained before entering the US and must be valid for the duration of the trip.

Some travelers may be required to present additional documents when entering the United States, in addition to their passport and visa. Travelers entering the United States by air, for example, may be required to show proof of onward travel, such as a return ticket. Those traveling by land into the United States may be asked to show proof of financial responsibility, such as a recent credit card statement.

Finally, when entering the United States, all visitors must show valid identification. A driver's license, state-issued ID card, or passport is acceptable. All documents must be in order and presented at the port of entry.

Finally, a valid passport, visa (for international travelers), and other necessary documents are required for travel to Las Vegas. It is critical for travelers to understand the documents required for entry and to ensure that all documents are current and valid. This will help to ensure a smooth and trouble-free travel experience.

Local Costumes and Etiquettes of Las Vegas

Las Vegas is a vibrant city with many different cultures and traditions. The city is well-known for its nightlife, casinos, and entertainment, but it also has a unique set of customs and etiquette. This guide will provide an overview of the local customs and etiquettes of Las Vegas, from dress codes to dining etiquette.

Clothing

It is critical to dress appropriately for the occasion in Las Vegas. In general, most occasions call for casual attire. Some of the city's more upscale establishments, on the other hand, may require more formal attire. Some casinos, for example, may require a collared shirt or a dress to enter. Furthermore, some nightlife and entertainment establishments may require more formal attire.

Bright colors and patterns are popular choices for local customs. Women typically wear dresses and skirts, while men may wear khakis and collared shirts.

Hats and other accessories are frequently worn to add a splash of personality.

Dining Manners

It is critical to follow local customs and etiquette whcn dining out in Las Vegas. When at the table, keep your hands above the table, avoid talking with your mouth full, and wait for everyone to be served before starting to eat. It is also customary to leave a small tip at the end of the meal.

It is polite to wait your turn when ordering and to avoid interrupting the server. Furthermore, it is critical to consider the menu and select items that are within your budget. Finally, it is customary to thank the server for their assistance.

Greetings

In Las Vegas, greetings differ depending on the situation. It is customary to extend a handshake and introduce yourself when meeting someone for the first time. Furthermore, when addressing someone, it is customary to use their full name.

When greeting someone you know, it is customary to give them a hug or a kiss on the cheek. Furthermore, when addressing someone, it is customary to use their first name.

Languages Spoken in Las Vegas

English is the official language of Las Vegas, and it is widely spoken and understood throughout the city. In fact, English is the most commonly used language in the United States, and Las Vegas is no exception.

However, due to its cosmopolitan nature, Las Vegas is also home to a variety of other languages, reflecting its inhabitants' diverse backgrounds and cultural traditions.

With a significant proportion of the population of Hispanic or Latino origin, Spanish is the second most commonly spoken language in Las Vegas. The US Census Bureau estimates that approximately 29% of Las Vegas residents speak Spanish at home. As a result, Spanish is an important language for businesses and organizations that want to serve the Hispanic community.

Tagalog, the national language of the Philippines, is also widely spoken in Las Vegas. There is a sizable Filipino community in Las Vegas, and many of its members speak Tagalog.

Chinese is also widely spoken in Las Vegas, reflecting the city's growing Chinese population.

Travel Phrases for Las Vegas

Here are some of the most common Las Vegas travel phrases you should know before you go.

"Where is the nearest casino?" - Casinos are one of the main attractions in Las Vegas, so knowing this phrase is a good idea. The Spanish equivalent is "Dónde está el casino más cercano?"

"How much do you want for this?" - Knowing the phrase "Cuánto cuesta esto?" is a great way to quickly find out how much something costs.

"Do you have any recommendations?" - When looking for places to visit, eat, or stay in Las

Vegas, this is a useful phrase to ask locals. ""¿Tiene alguna recomendación?" is the Spanish translation.

"I'm looking for a hotel" - Use this phrase if you're looking for a place to stay in Las Vegas. "Estoy buscando un hotel" is the Spanish translation.

"Where is the nearest ATM?" - Knowing this phrase is essential because having cash on hand is always a good idea in Las Vegas. The Spanish translation is "Dónde está el cajero automático más cercano?"

"Can you help me?" - You can use this phrase if you require assistance. "Puedes ayudarme?" is the Spanish equivalent.

"What is the best way to get around?" This phrase is useful if you're looking for the best way to get around Las Vegas. "Cuál es la mejor manera de moverse por aqu?" is the Spanish translation.

"Where is the nearest pharmacy?" - Knowing the location of the nearest pharmacy can be extremely useful in an emergency. "Dónde está la farmacia más cercana?" is the Spanish translation.

Knowing these essential travel phrases for Las Vegas will help you make the most of your trip. If you remember these phrases, you'll be able to communicate with the locals and make the most of your time in the city.

Conclusion

Final Thoughts and Recommendations for Travelers

Millions of tourists visit Las Vegas each year to enjoy the city's distinct blend of entertainment, glitz, and excitement, making it one of the world's most well-known tourist destinations. In this vibrant city, there are numerous sights and activities to enjoy, including the well-known Las Vegas Strip and its numerous casinos, eateries, and nightclubs.

Here are some parting words of wisdom and tips for anyone thinking about visiting Las Vegas.

First and foremost, keep in mind that Las Vegas is a desert city, and it can get very hot there during the summer.

Visitors are advised to visit in the spring or fall when the weather is more pleasant, or to bring sunscreen, a hat, and plenty of water if visiting in the summer.

Although the Las Vegas Strip is the center of the city's entertainment scene, there is much more to see and discover than casinos and flashing lights. Visitors should take the time to explore some of the other interesting areas and destinations off the Strip, such as the Neon Museum, the Arts District, and the Fremont Street Experience.

Las Vegas has a wide range of lodging options, from opulent resorts to more affordable hotels. Because prices and availability vary greatly depending on the season, travelers should do their research and make reservations for their lodging in advance.

Las Vegas is well-known for its first-rate dining and nightlife, with a plethora of restaurants and bars serving a wide range of cuisines and providing various forms of entertainment. From celebrity chefs to regional favorites, there is something for every taste and budget. It's important to remember, however, that you should never drink and drive.

In terms of entertainment, Las Vegas is well-known for its shows, concerts, and performances by some of the biggest names in comedy, music, and theater. Tickets should be purchased in advance because shows frequently sell out.

Last but not least, remember that Las Vegas is a city that never sleeps and that there is always something going on. There is never a dull moment in this exciting and dynamic city, whether you are gambling, shopping, or simply people-watching.

Made in the USA
Coppell, TX
10 June 2023

17925179R10049